Super Simple Designs

An Adult Coloring Book with Easier Designs for Easier Coloring.

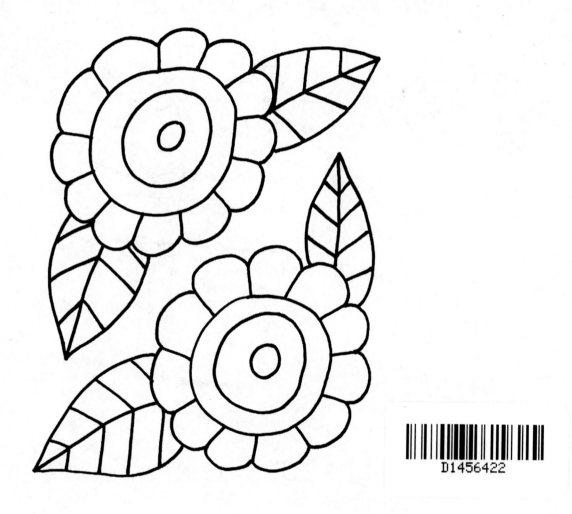

Super Simple Drawings
by Kimberly Garvey

Kimberlygarvey.com

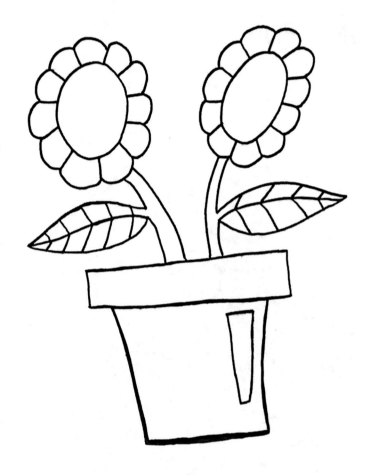

This book is dedicated to everyone who has supported me on my coloring book journey.

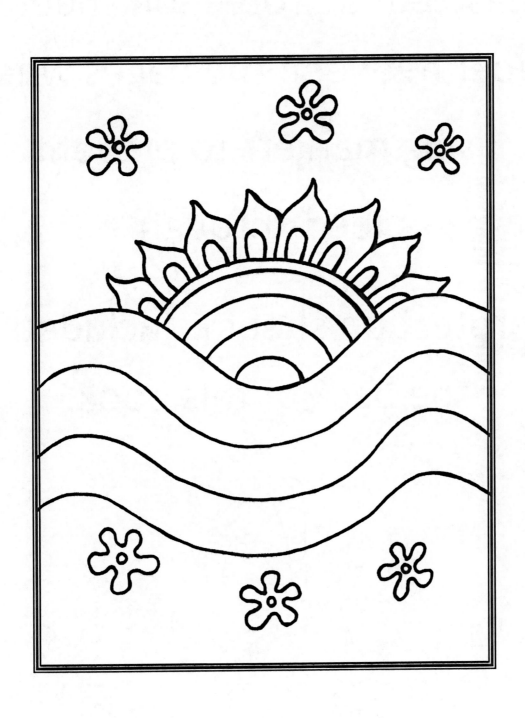

WARNING!!!!

Please put a protection sheet of paper between the pages when using markers to prevent bleed-through.

A protection sheet is included at the back of this book.

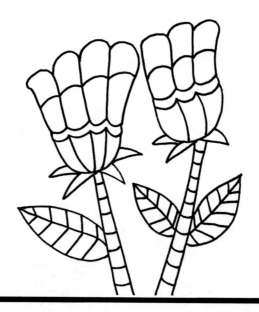

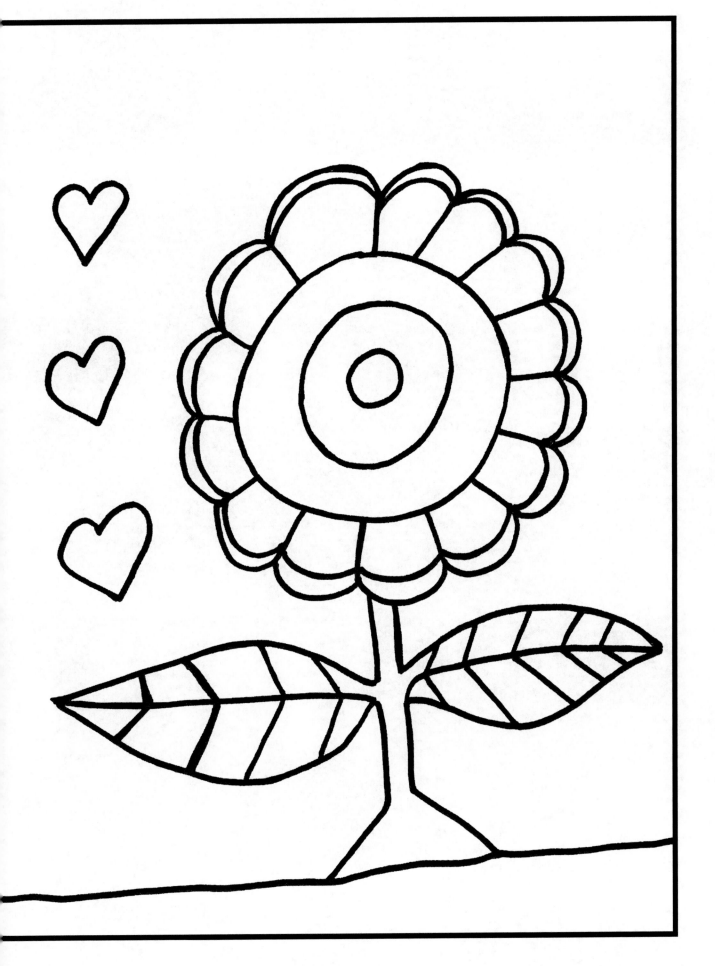

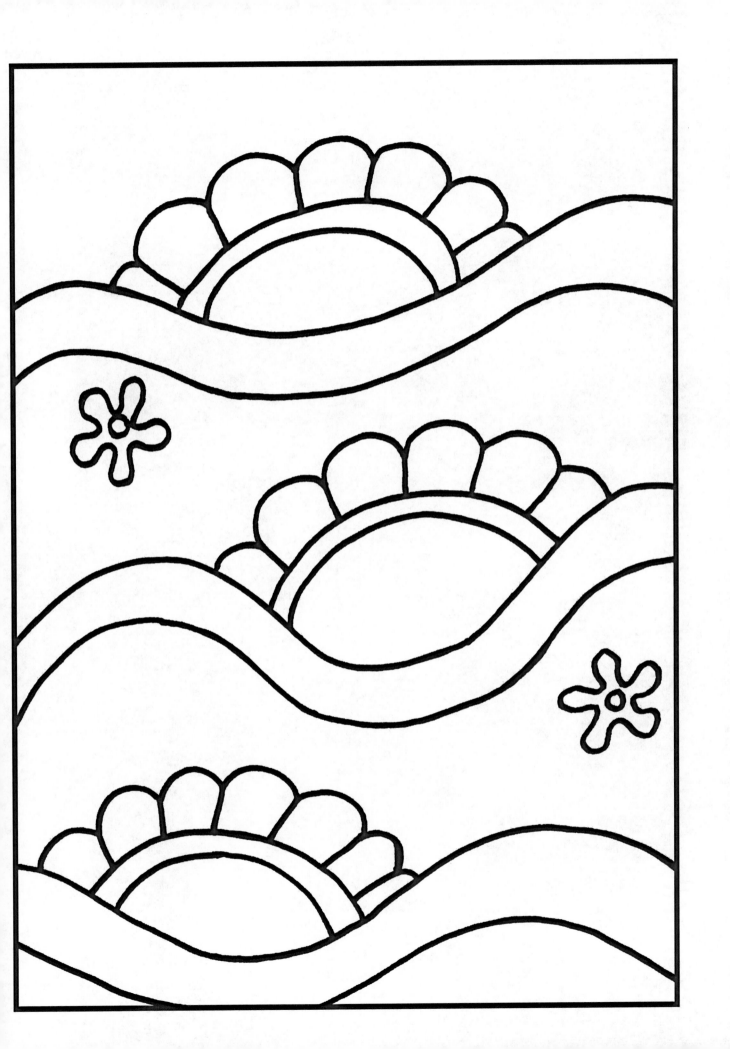

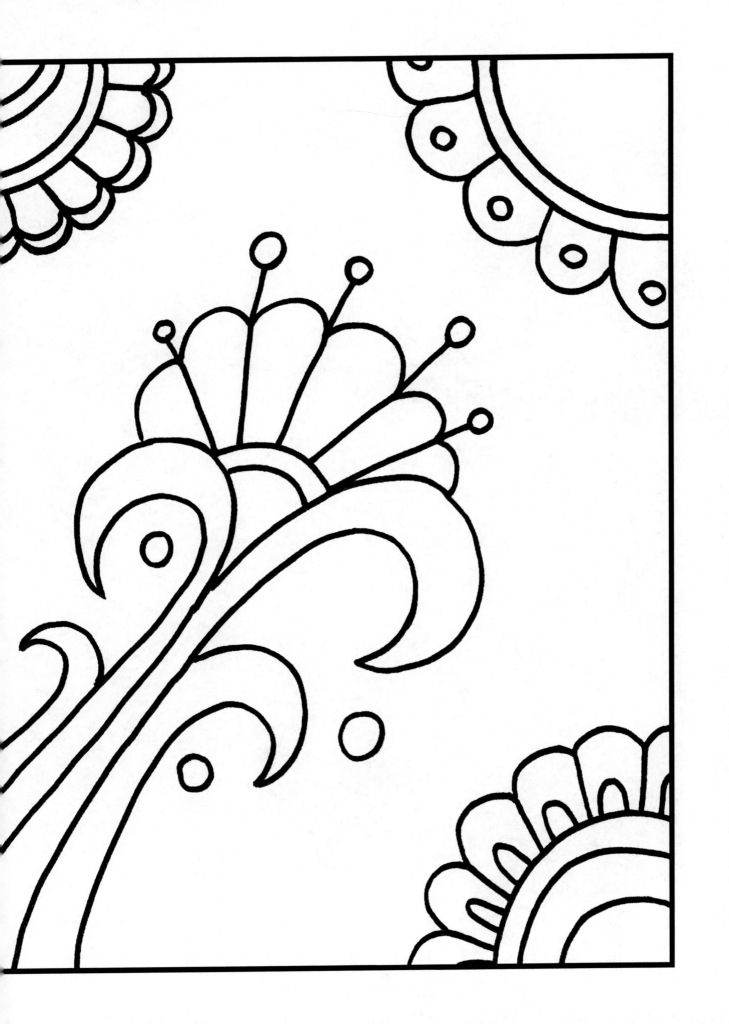

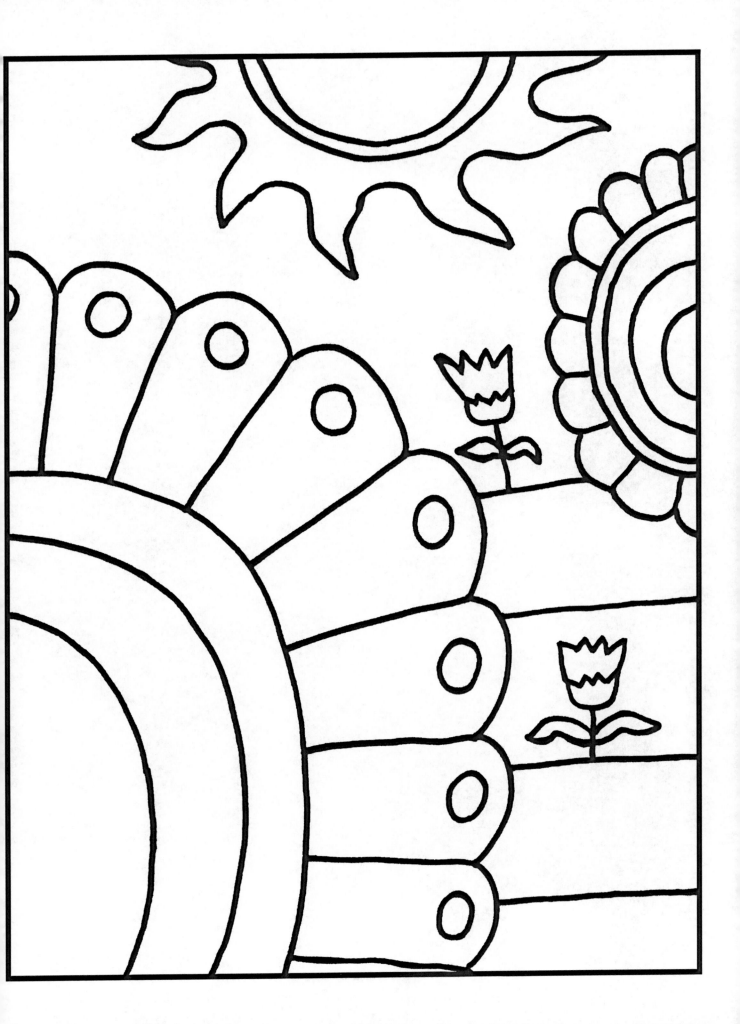

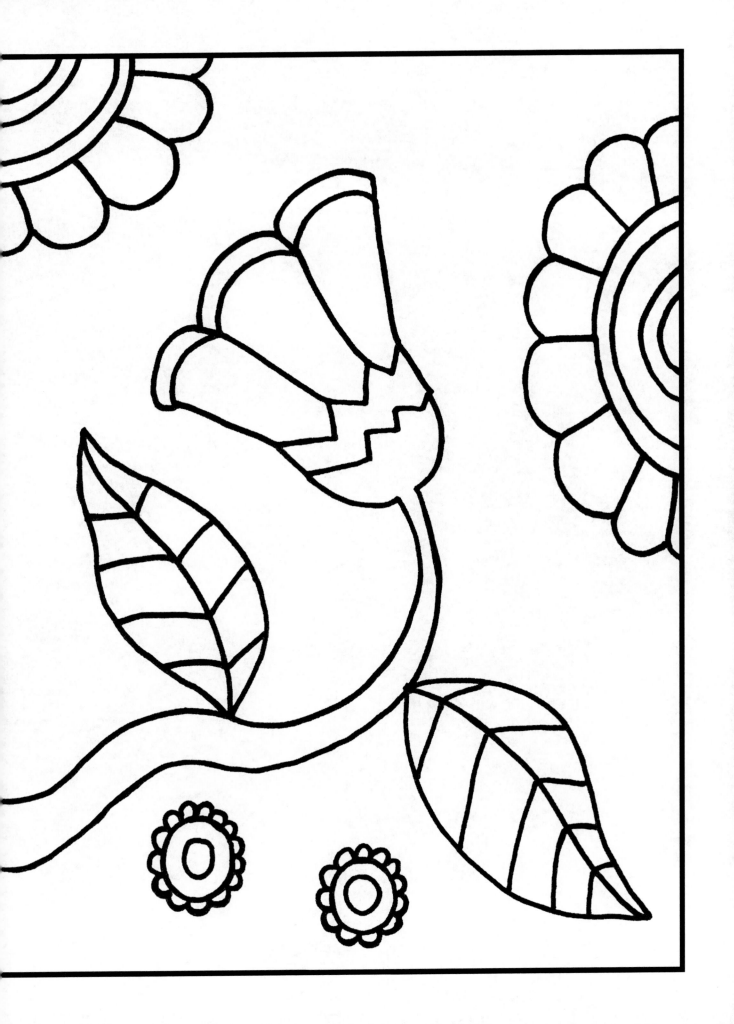

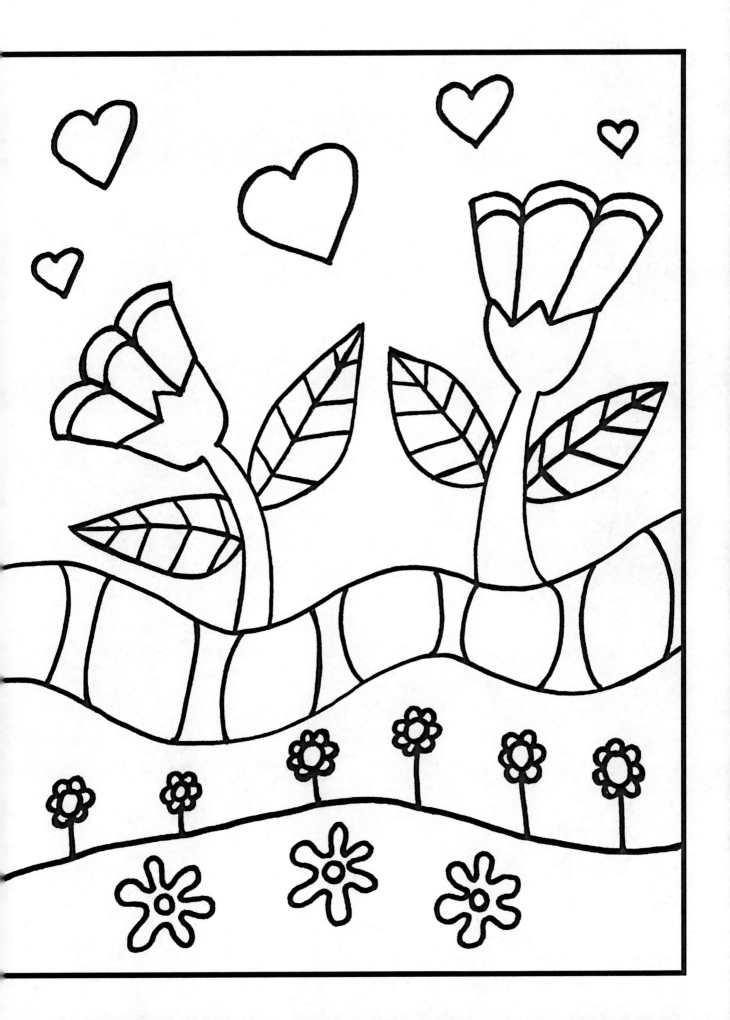

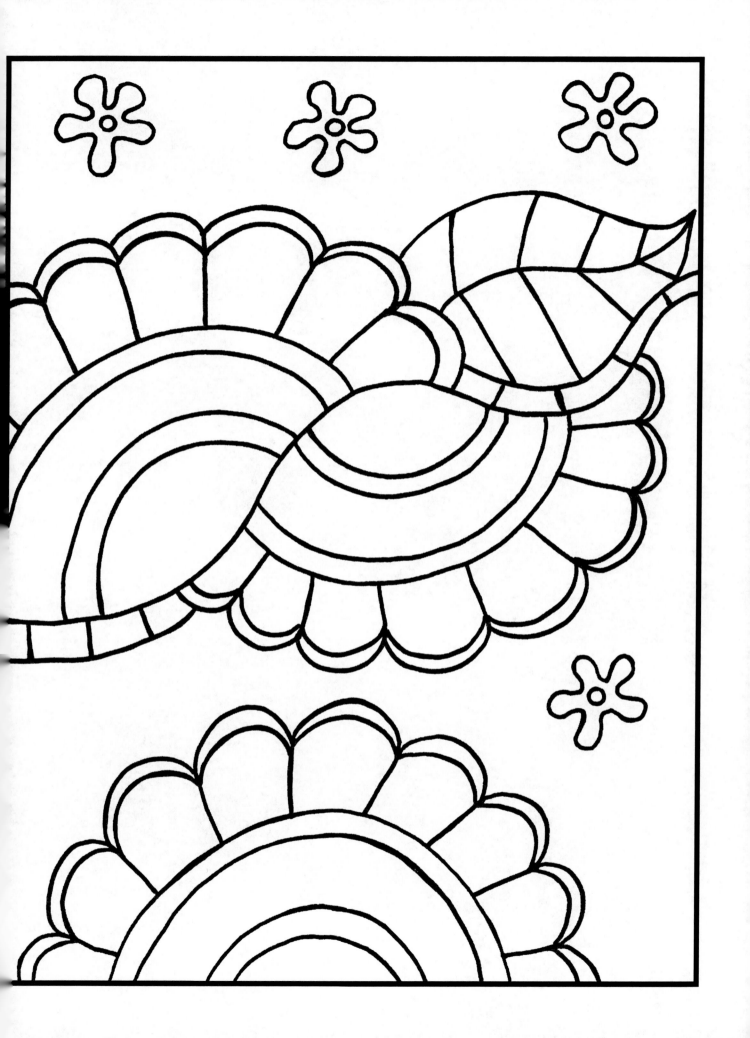

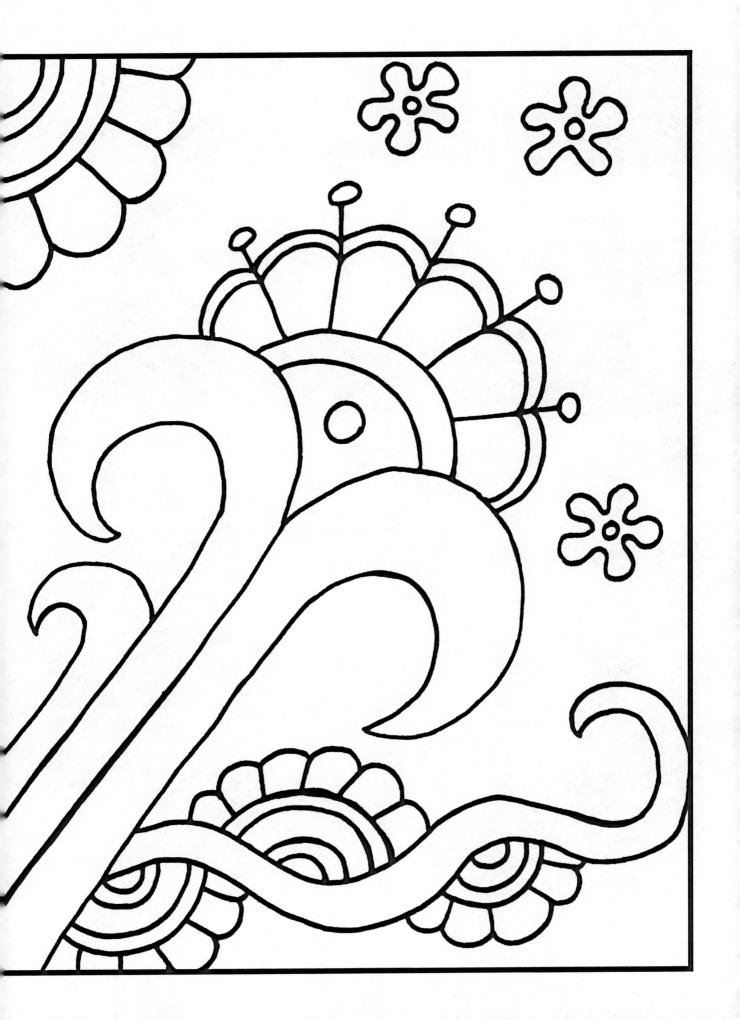

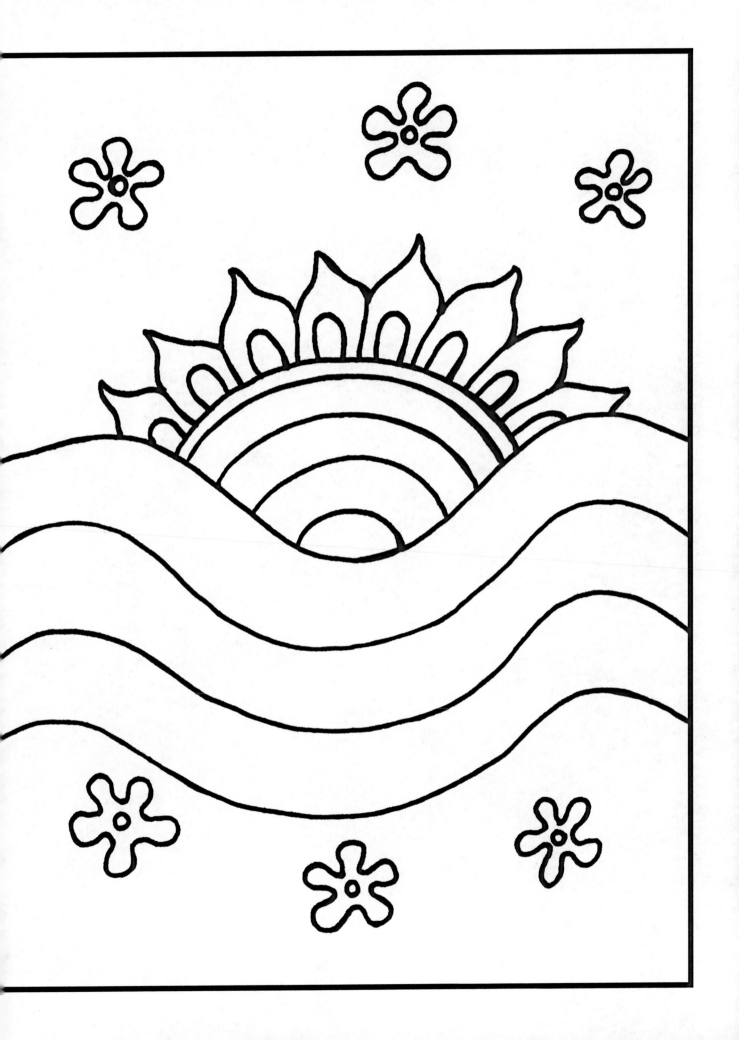

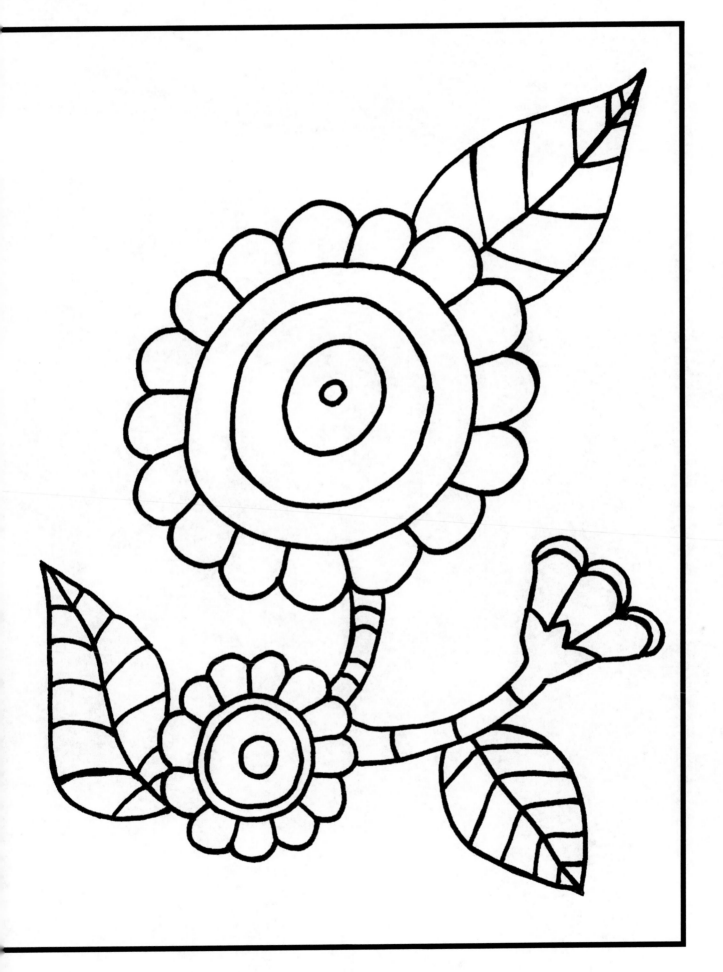

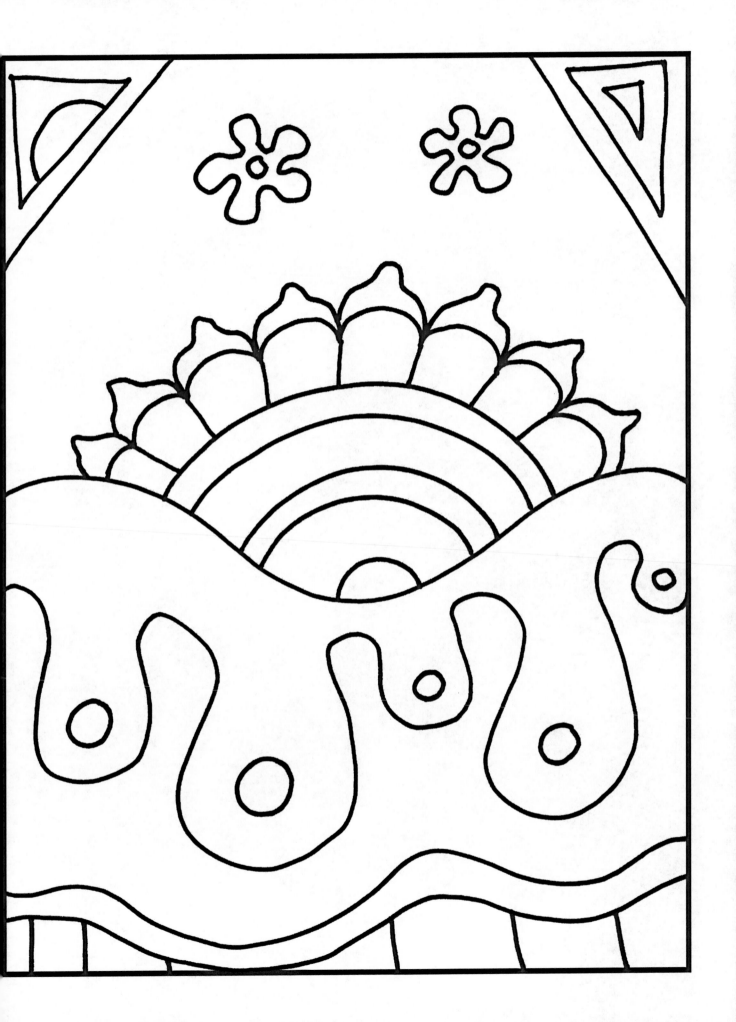

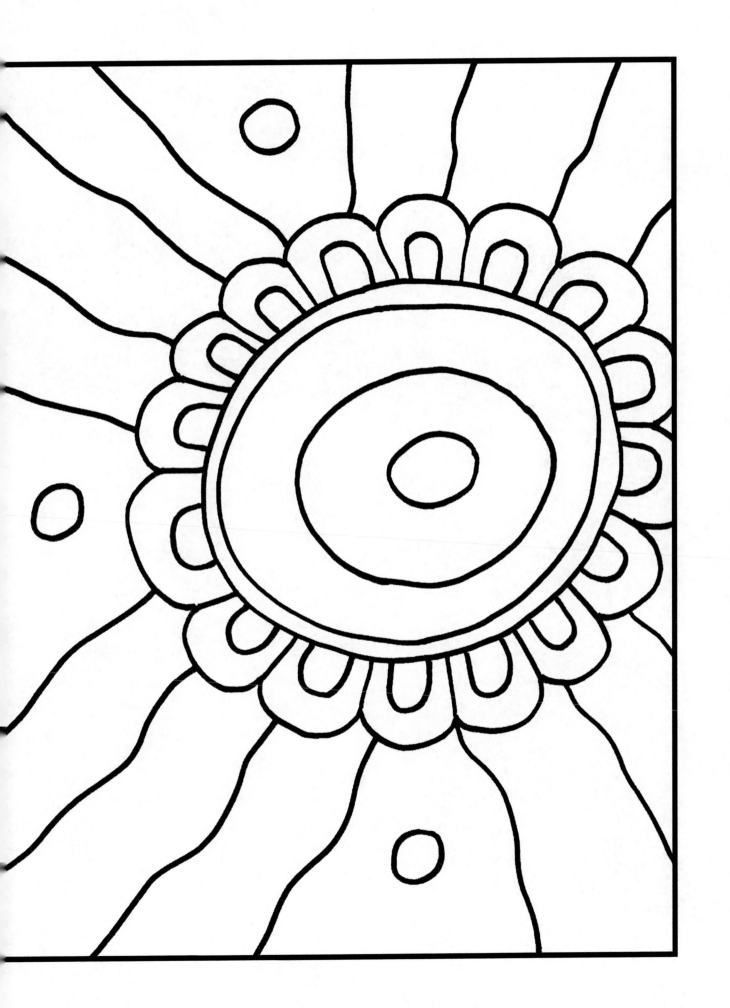

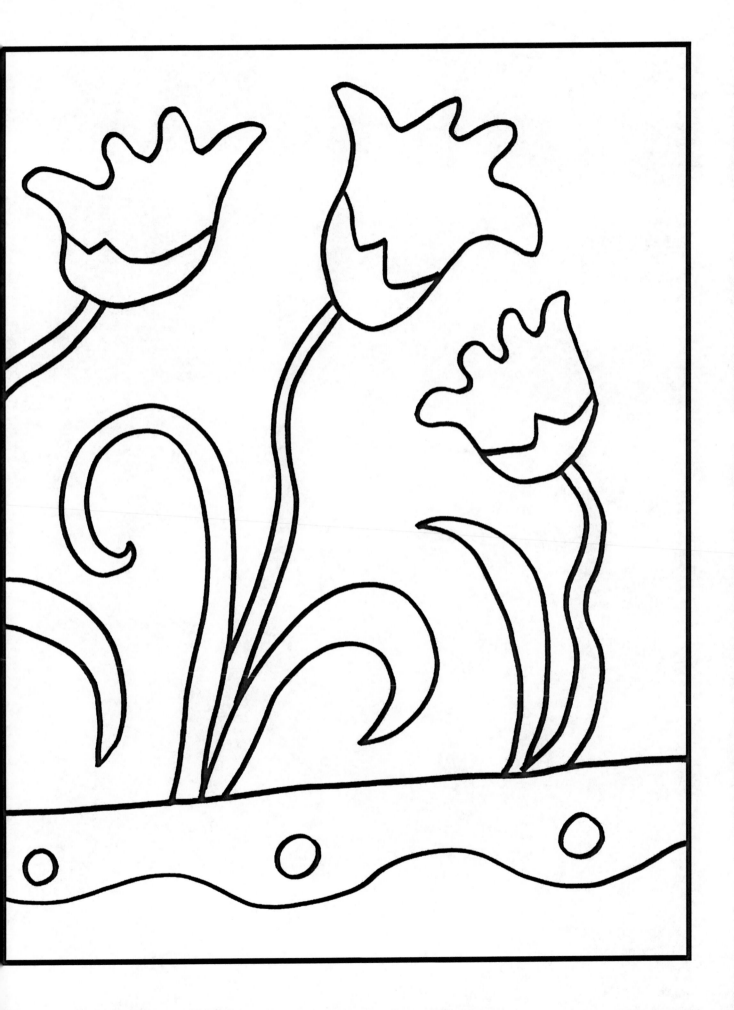

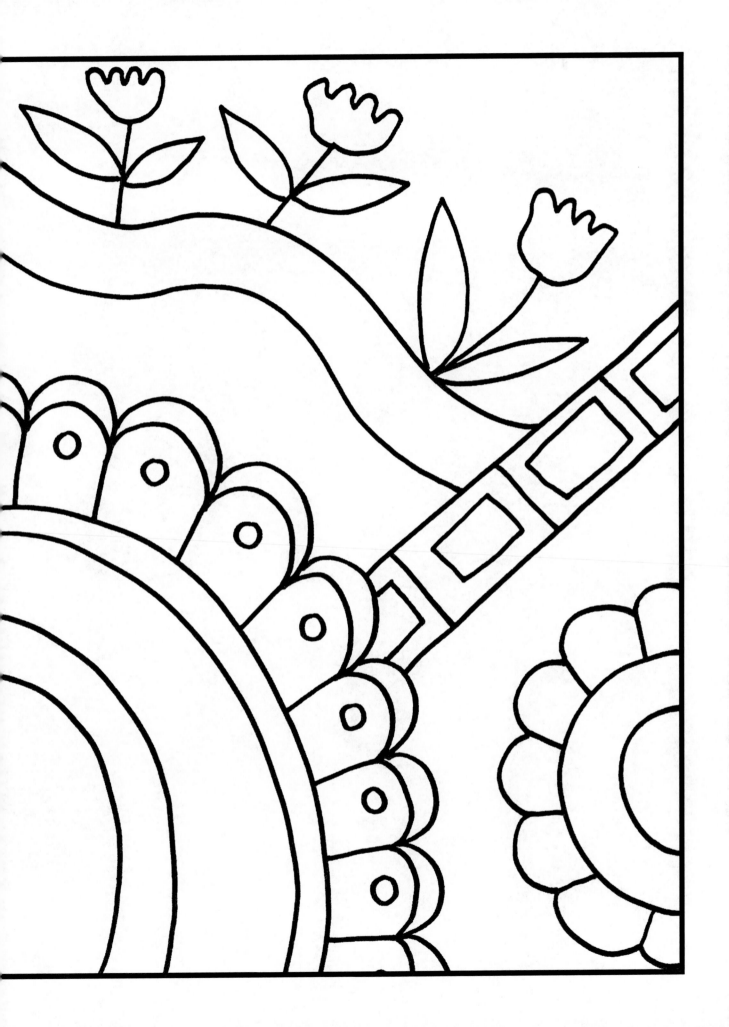

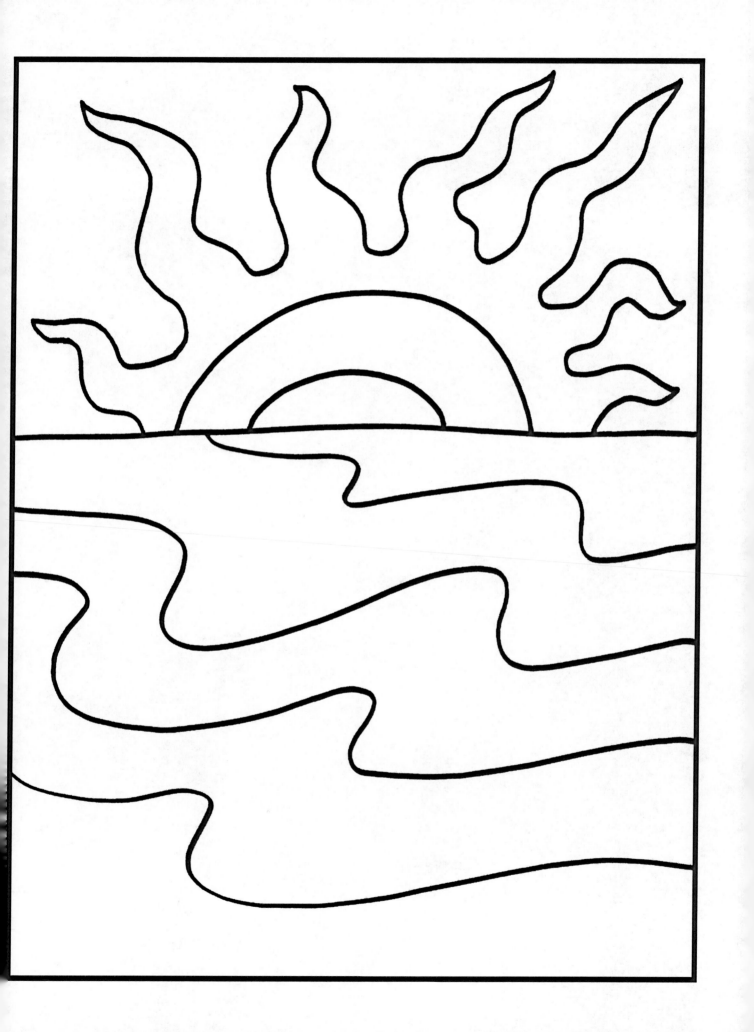

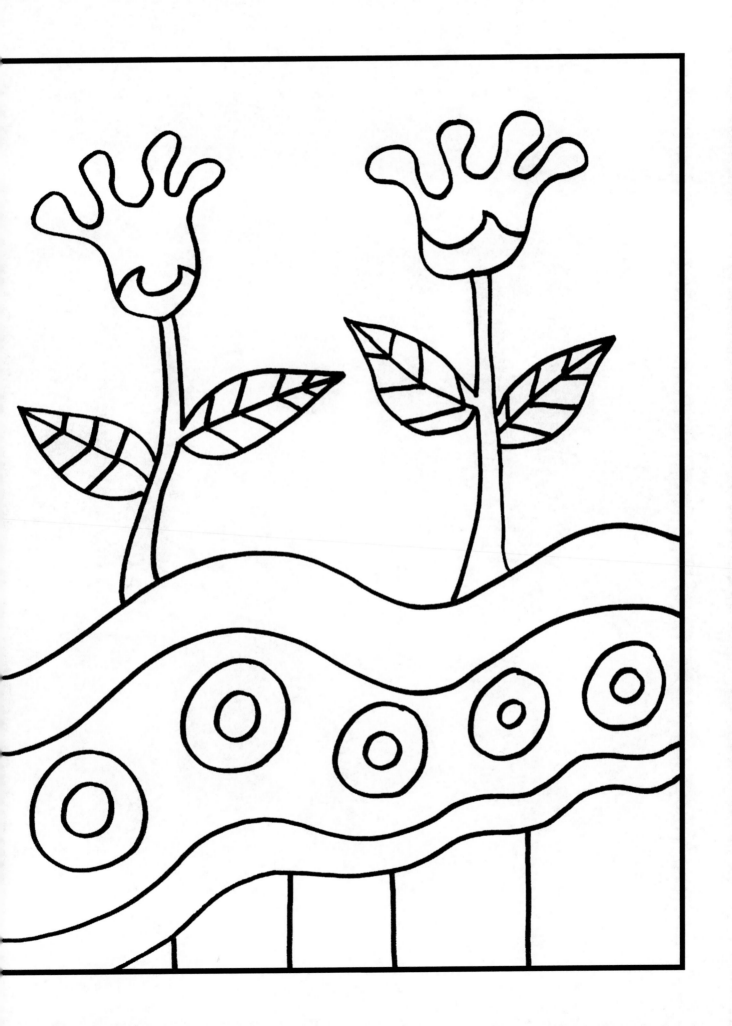

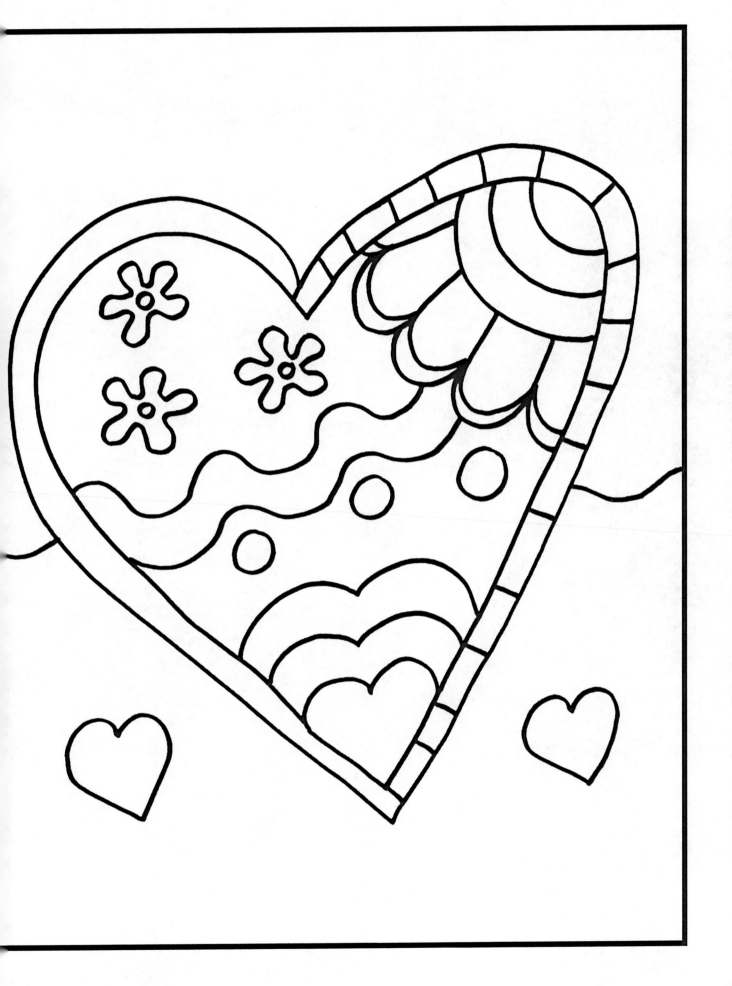

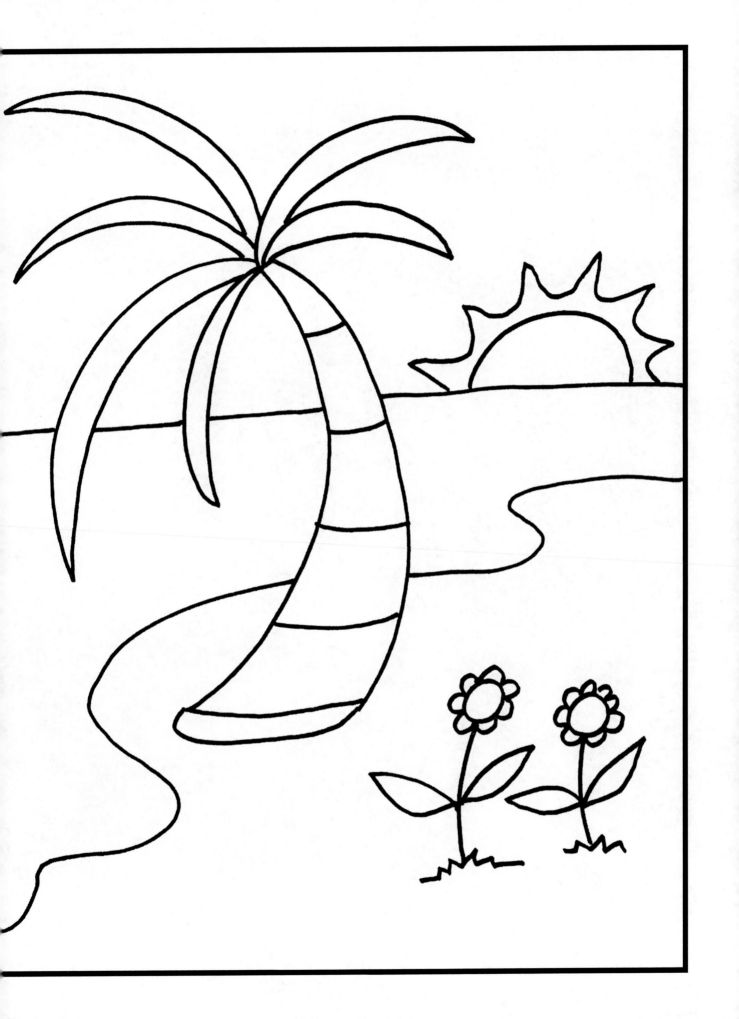

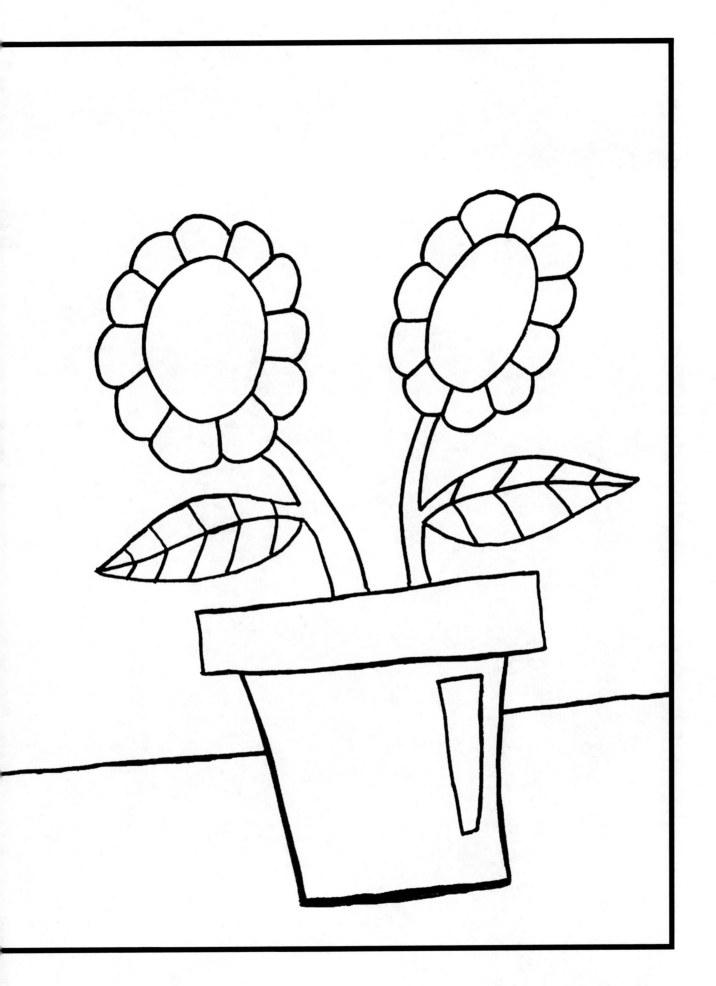

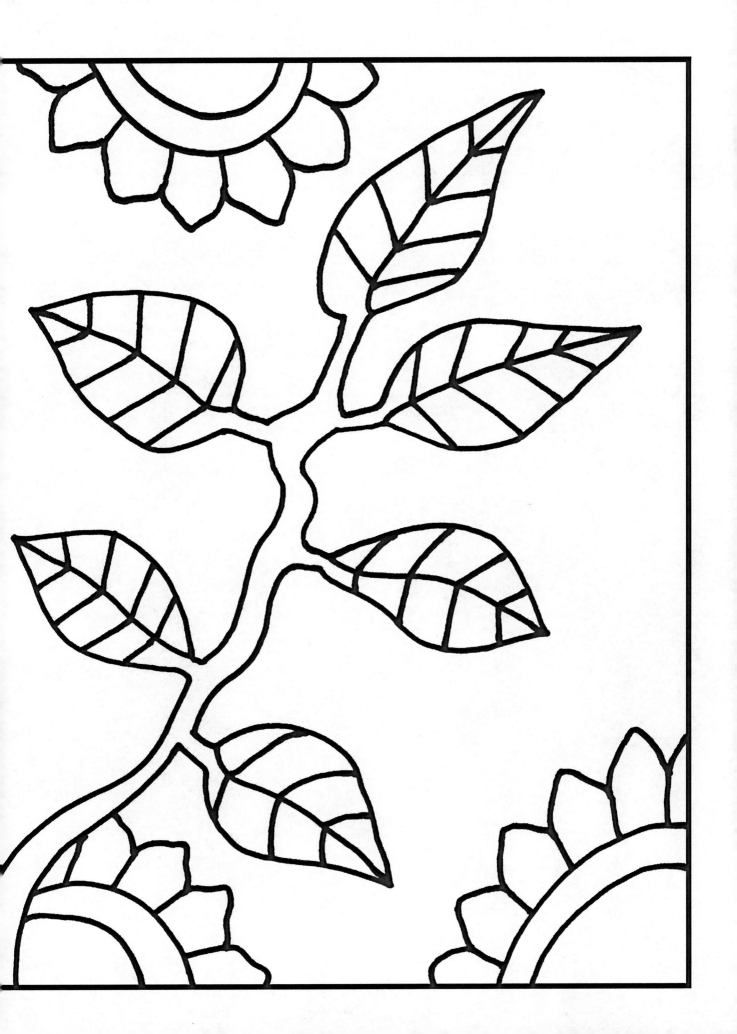

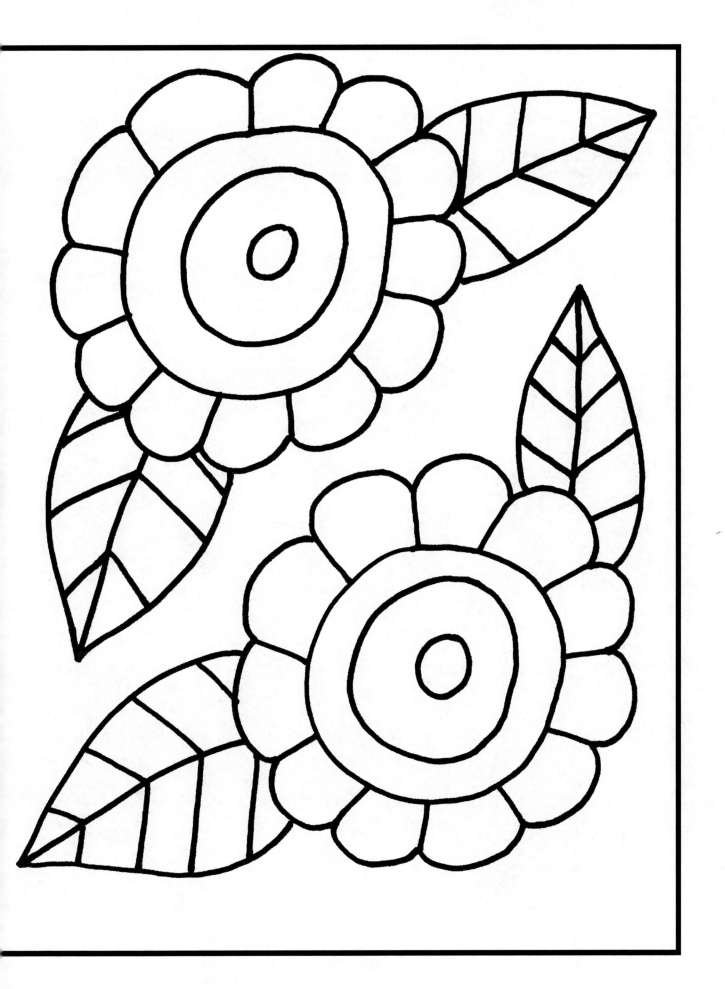

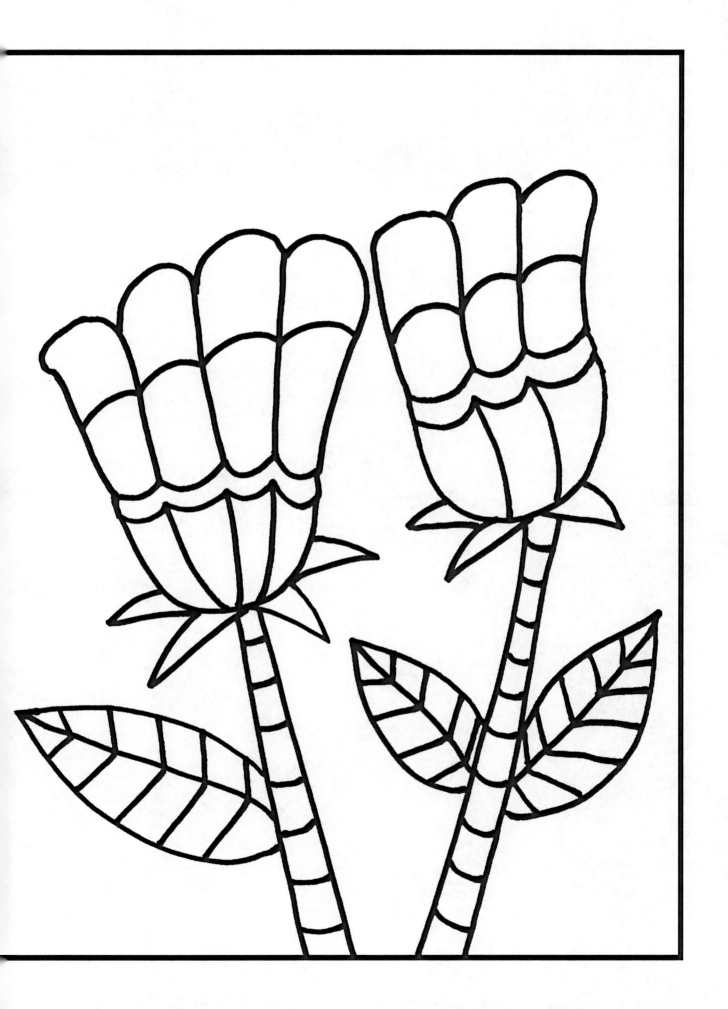

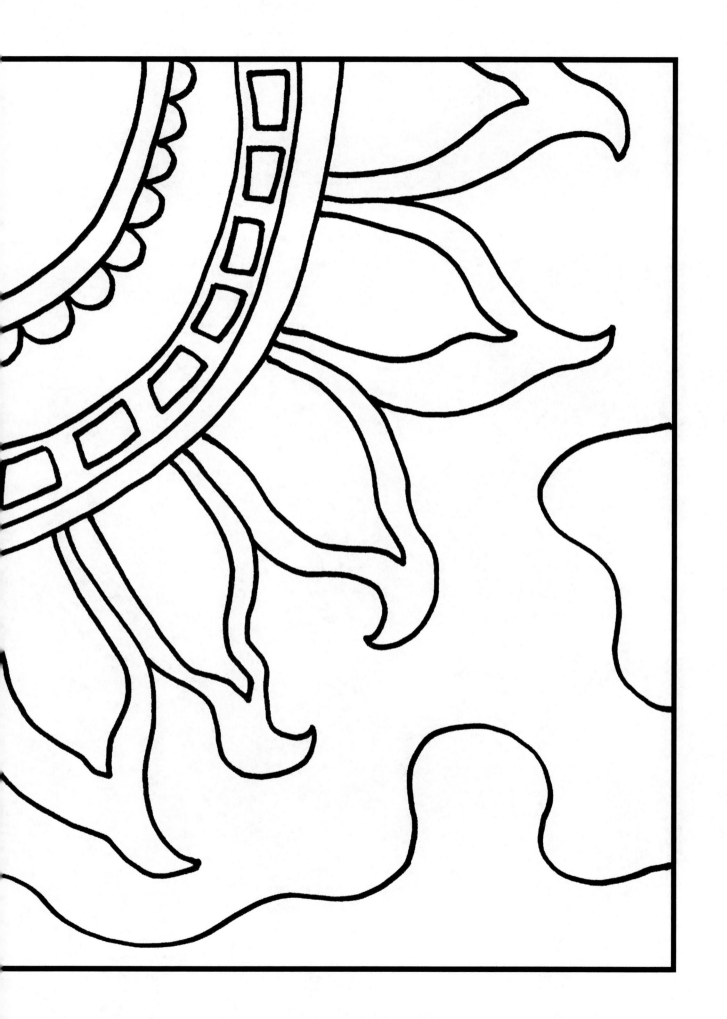

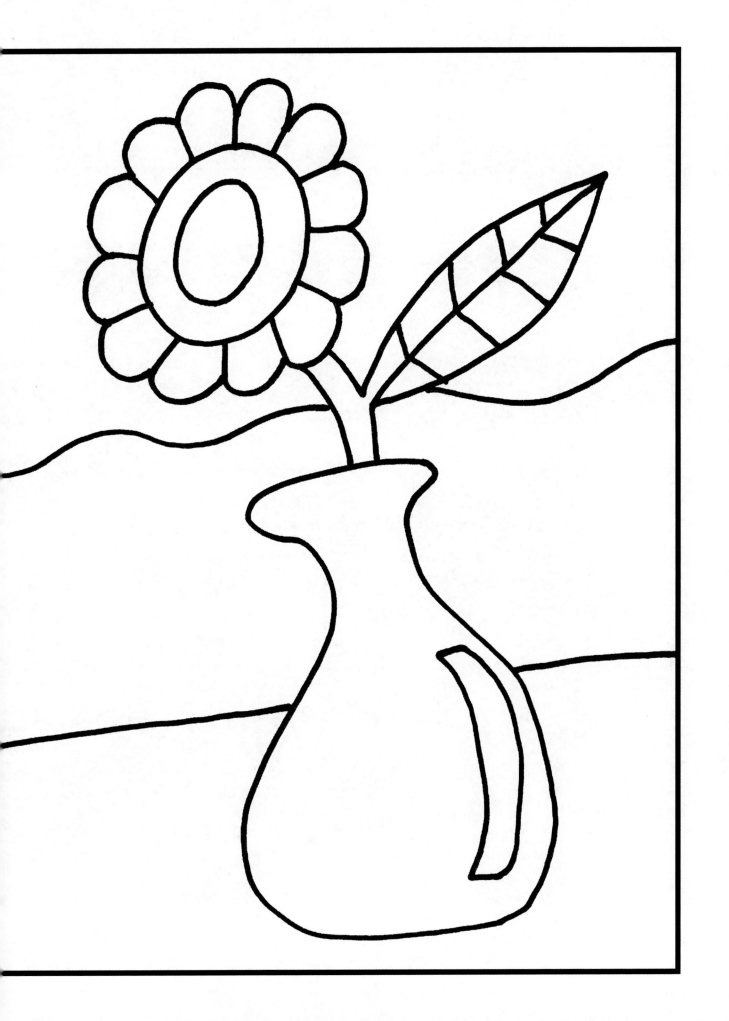

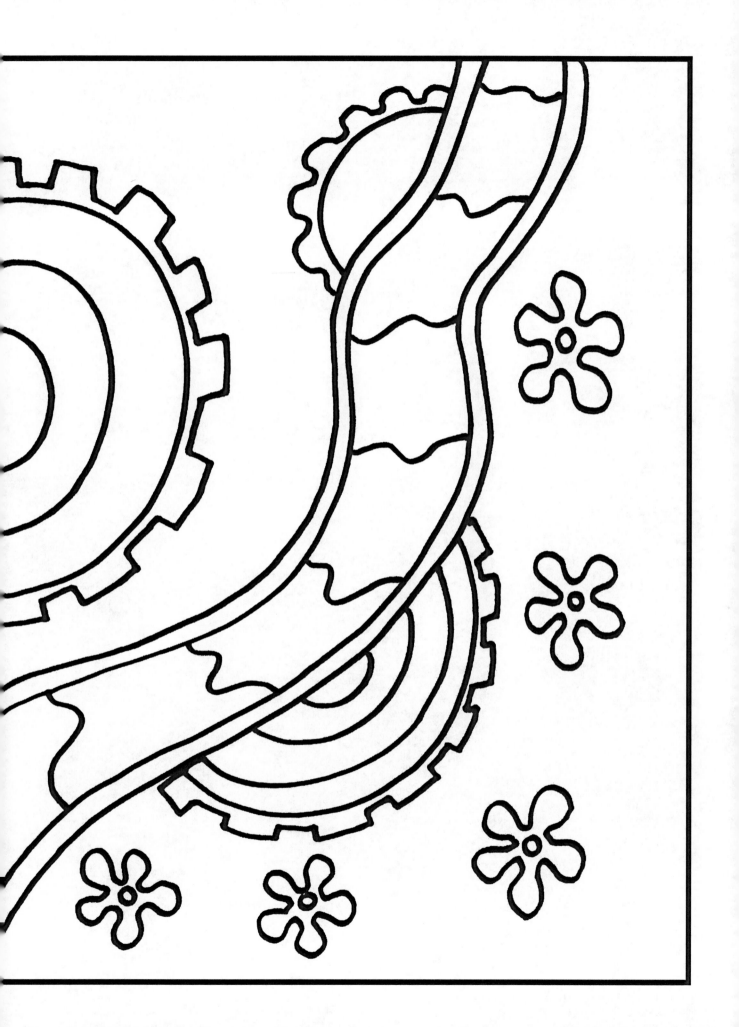

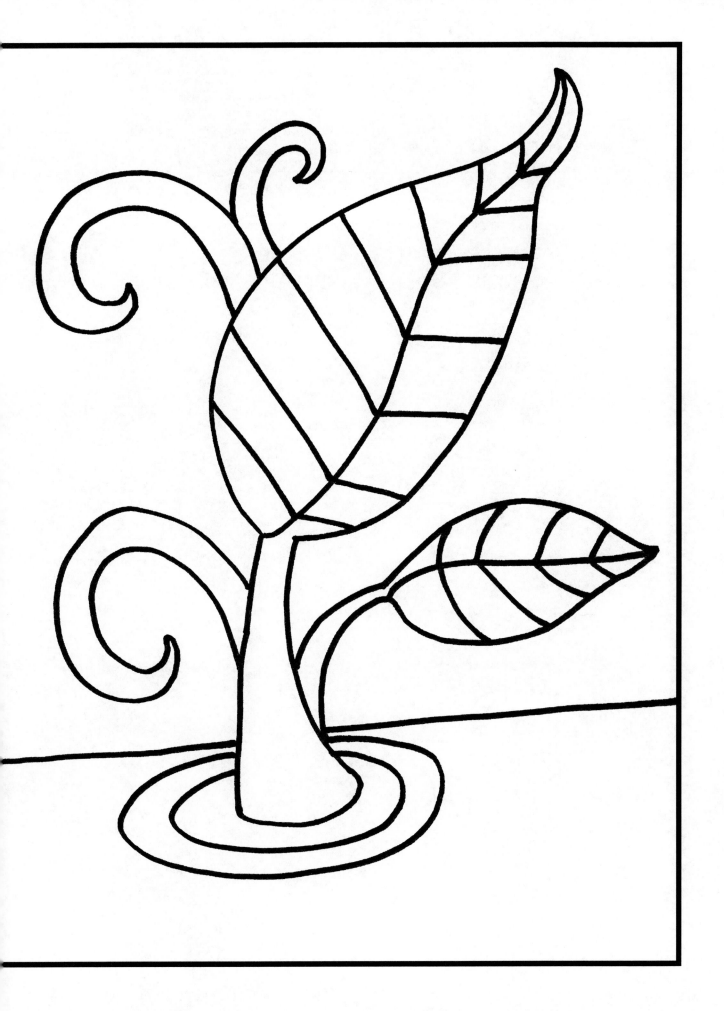

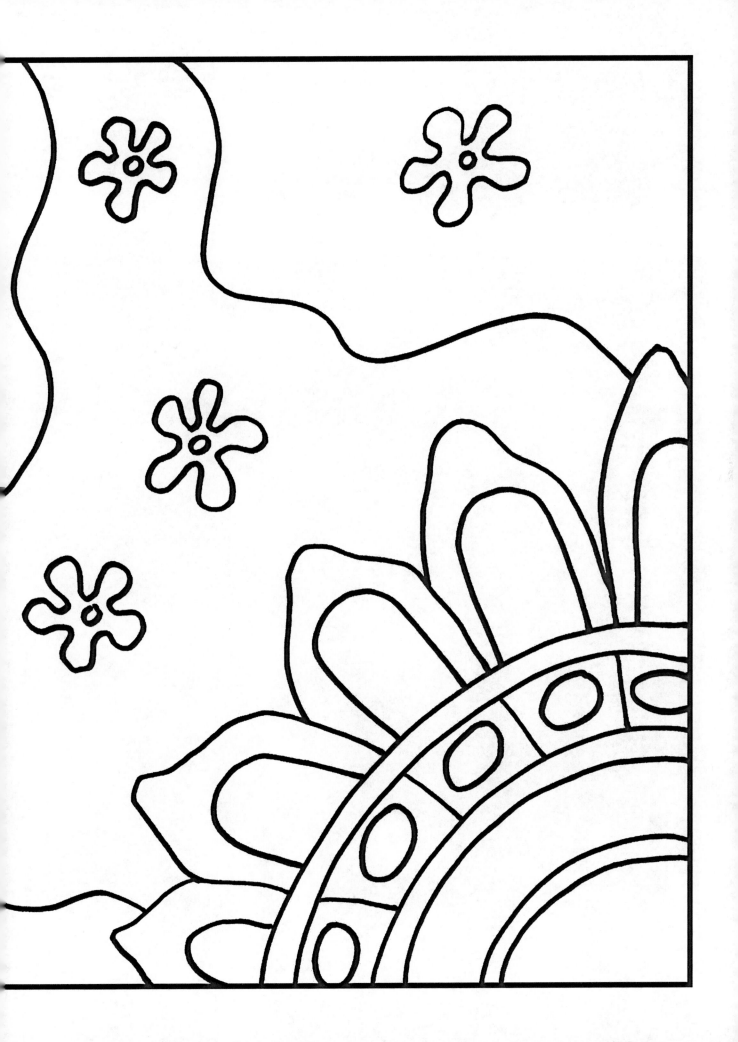

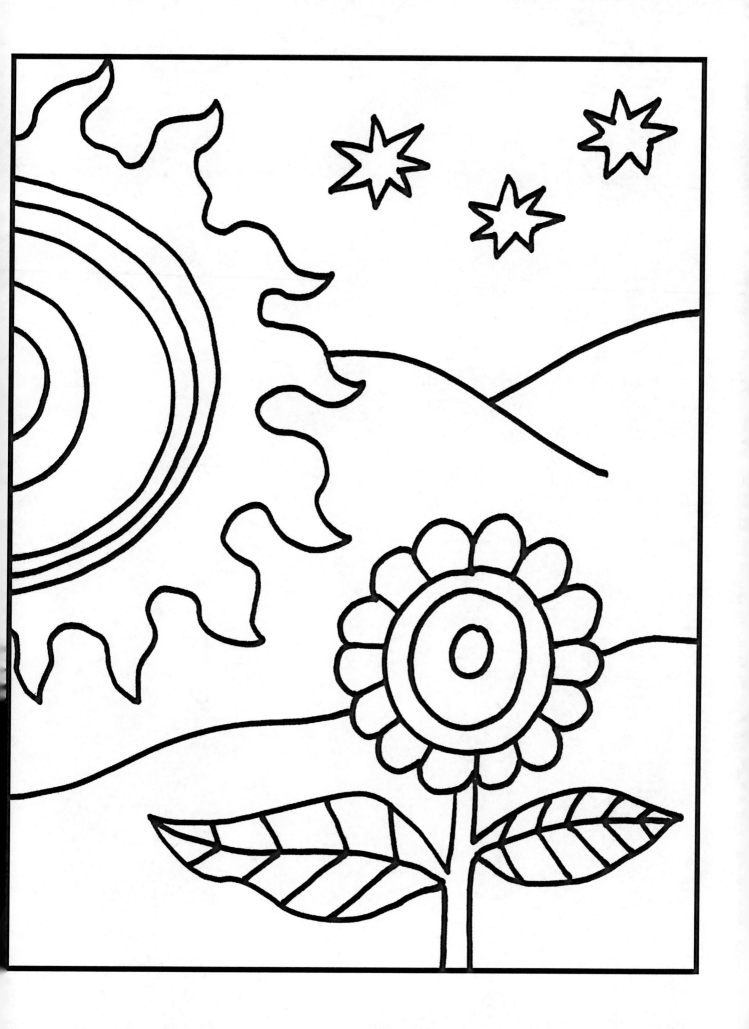

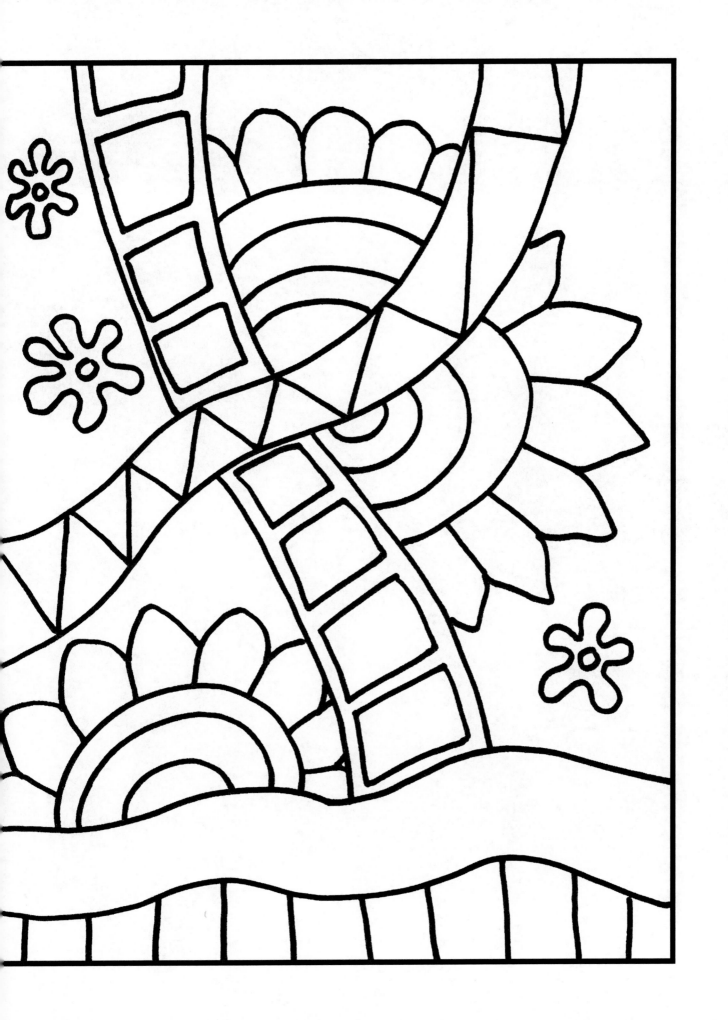

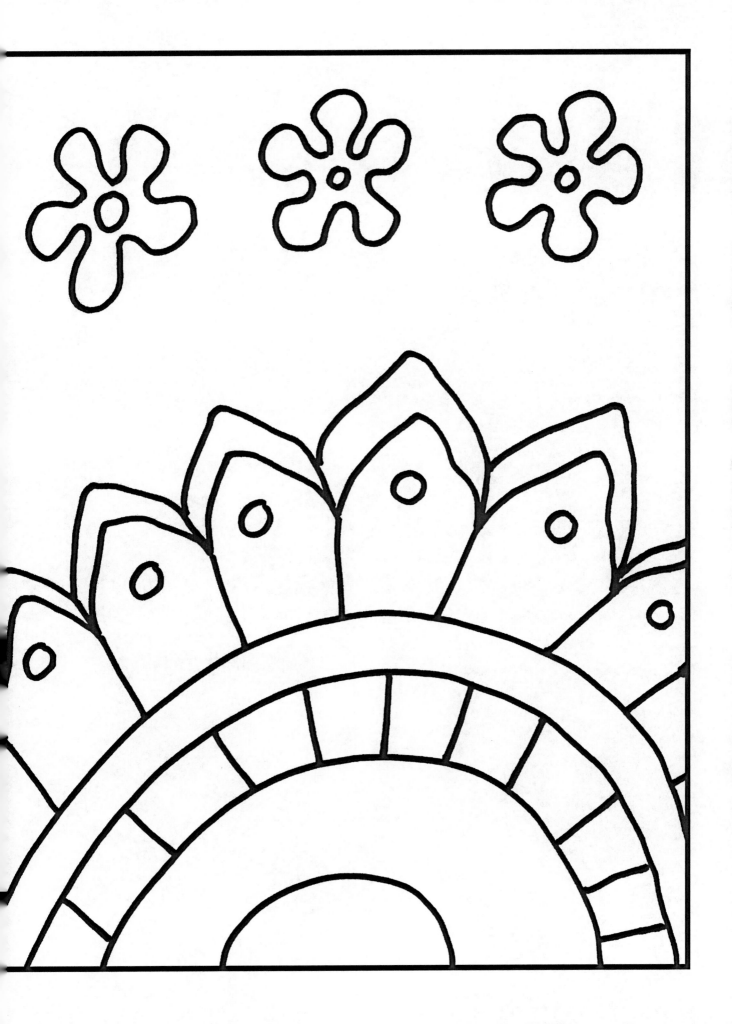

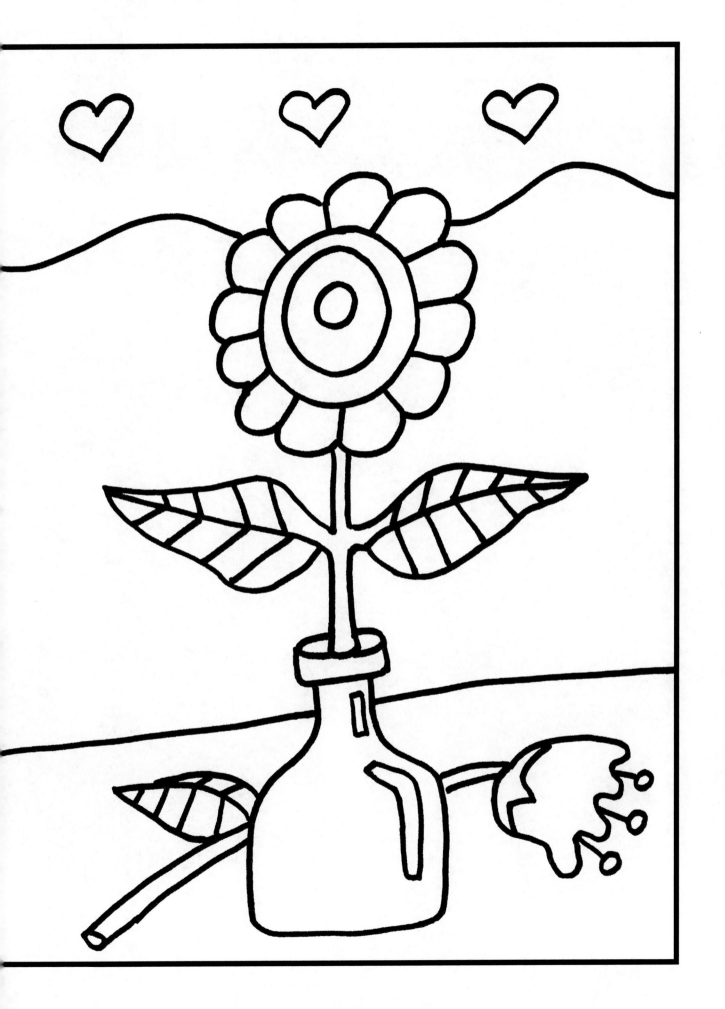

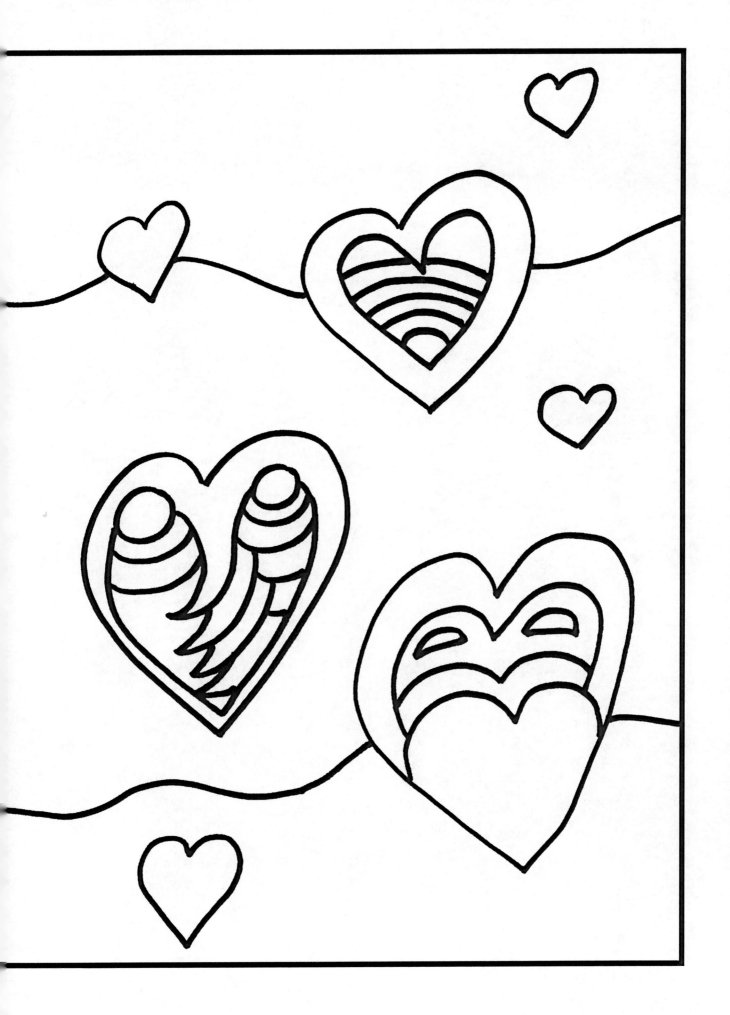

ALSO AVAILABLE BY KIMBERLY GARVEY

- **Strange Designs** - An adult coloring book for everyone.

- **Strange Little Designs** - A mini/travel adult coloring book.

- **Simple Designs** - An adult coloring book with easier pages.

- **Simple Designs II** - Another adult coloring book with easier pages.

- **Magical Daydreams** - An adult coloring book for everyone.

- **It's Complicated** - A challenging. more detailed book for the daring colorists.

- **The Fox Book** - A foxy coloring book for everyone.

KIMBERLYGARVEY.COM

PROTECTION SHEET

Place this page between coloring pages when using markers to prevent bleed-through.

KIMBERLYGARVEY.COM

CPSIA information can be obtained
at www.ICGtesting.com
Printed in the USA
LVOW09s1849140517

534495LV00022B/370/P

9 781519 111140